Crabapples

Giraffes

Bobbie Kalman & Greg Nickles

Crabtree Publishing Company

Crabapples

created by Bobbie Kalman

For Troy Kozma, in windy Chicago

Editor-in-Chief
Bobbie Kalman

Writing team
Bobbie Kalman
Greg Nickles

Managing editor
Lynda Hale

Editors
Niki Walker
Petrina Gentile

Consultant
Peter Ross Croskery

Computer design
Lynda Hale
Lucy DeFazio

Color separations and film
Dot 'n Line Image Inc.

Illustrations
Barbara Bedell: pages 7, 16-17

Photographs
Animals Animals: David C. Fritts: page 21 (bottom);
  Anup & Manoj Shah: pages 12-13
Frank S. Balthis: page 31
Fredrik D. Bodin/Offshoot: page 30
Wolfgang Kaehler: title page, pages 18-19, 24, 25, 26, 27, 29
James A. Martin/Offshoot: cover
Photo Researchers, Inc.: Nigel Dennis: page 8 (top);
  Gregory G. Dimijian: pages 14, 19, 22 (all), 23;
  David Hosking: page 8 (bottom); M. Philip Kahl, Jr.: page 21 (top);
  Paolo Koch: page 6; William & Marcia Levy: page 28 (bottom);
  Renee Lynn: page 28 (top); Anthony Mercieca Photo: page 9 (inset)
Tom Stack & Associates: Thomas Kitchin: pages 4-5; Joe McDonald:
  page 9; John Shaw: page 15; Roy Toft: page 10
Dave Taylor: pages 7, 20

Printer
Worzalla Publishing Company

Crabtree Publishing Company

350 Fifth Avenue
Suite 3308
New York
N.Y. 10118

360 York Road, RR 4,
Niagara-on-the-Lake,
Ontario, Canada
L0S 1J0

73 Lime Walk
Headington
Oxford OX3 7AD
United Kingdom

Cataloging in Publication Data
Kalman, Bobbie
  Giraffes

(Crabapples)
Includes index.

ISBN 0-86505-641-2 (library bound) ISBN 0-86505-741-9 (pbk.)
This book examines the biology, behavior, and habitats of the
African mammal known for its long neck.

1. Giraffes - Juvenile literature. I. Nickles, Greg, 1969-
II. Title. III. Series: Kalman, Bobbie, Crabapples.

QL737.U56K34 1997   j599.638   LC 97-5140
                                                      CIP

What is in this book?

What is a giraffe?

Giraffes are **mammals**. People are mammals too. Mammals are animals that have hair or fur. They are **warm-blooded**. Their body temperature stays the same, no matter how warm or cold their surroundings are. A few female mammals lay eggs, but most bear **live young**. Newborn mammals drink their mother's milk.

Giraffes are the tallest animals in the world. Females, or **cows**, are 14 feet (4 meters) tall. Males, or **bulls**, are up to 17 feet (5 meters) tall. How tall are you?

Where do giraffes live?

Scientists believe that giraffes and their ancestors once lived in many parts of Africa, Europe, and Asia. Today, giraffes live only in some parts of Africa.

They spend most of their time on open, grassy plains or in areas with a few trees. In these places, it is easy for a giraffe to see an enemy and have time to escape.

Unlike many other animals, giraffes spend little time around water holes, which are dangerous places for them. An enemy can easily attack a giraffe while it is kneeling to drink. It is difficult for a kneeling giraffe to stand up quickly and escape.

Giraffe food

Giraffes are **herbivores**, or plant-eaters, but sometimes they chew on bones to get **minerals**. Giraffes spend most of their time **browsing**, or nibbling on leaves and twigs.

Giraffes like the buds and leaves of the acacia tree best. They also eat from other trees and bushes. These foods give giraffes most of the water their bodies need, but they do stop for a drink once in awhile.

A giraffe swallows most of its food whole. The food passes into its stomach, where it is broken down into soft balls of **cud**. When the giraffe is resting, it coughs up its cud, rechews the half-digested food, and swallows it again.

"Just chewing my cud!"

9

A giraffe's body

The giraffe's body is well suited to finding and eating food. Its long legs and neck help it reach buds and leaves high up in the trees, where other animals cannot reach. A giraffe also has a long tongue that it uses to grasp branches and strip them of leaves. The tongue is dark at the tip to protect it from sunburn.

The tongue is 15 inches (38 cm) long.

The horns are mostly bone and are covered with fur. Some giraffes have as many as five horns.

Giraffes have excellent eyesight. Their senses of hearing and smell may be the same as a human's.

The neck is over 6 feet (2 meters) long.

The tail can be more than 6 feet (2 meters) long. The hair at the end of the tail helps swish away insects.

The front legs and shoulders are very strong and help the giraffe run quickly.

Each hoof is as wide as this page.

What a neck!

A giraffe's neck is longer than that of any other animal. Not only is the neck long, but it is also very muscular and flexible.

A giraffe has seven neck bones, just as humans do, but the giraffe's bones are much larger. Giraffes also have extra-large lungs to pump air up and down their long windpipe. Their heart is huge because it has to pump blood all the way up to their head.

Scientists think that giraffes have special **valves** in their neck. A valve is a flap of skin in a blood vessel that helps control the flow of blood. If the giraffe's brain received too much or not enough blood, the giraffe would get dizzy. When the neck is upright, the valves may help push blood up to the brain. When the giraffe lowers its head, the valves stop blood in the neck from rushing to the giraffe's head.

13

Lots of spots

A giraffe's body is covered by a layer of fur that is almost an inch (2.5 cm) thick. Scientists believe the thick coat protects the giraffe from the hot sun. Young giraffes often have spots that are lighter in color than those of adults. The spots darken as the giraffes get older.

Spot patterns range from **irregular** to **reticulated**. The giraffes on the opposite page have irregular patterns on their coat. Irregular spots look jagged, and the cream-colored lines between them are wide. The giraffe on the right has a reticulated coat. Its spots are smooth-edged, and the lines between them are thin.

No two giraffes have identical spots on their coat. Giraffes from the same area of Africa, however, have similar spot patterns. The patterns may act as **camouflage** by helping giraffes hide from predators. The spots blend in with trees and make giraffes hard to see when they are standing still.

Giraffe family

Giraffes belong to a family whose members are called **giraffids**. The okapi is the only other giraffid. Giraffes and okapis are related to other animals with hooves, such as deer, antelopes, goats, sheep, and cattle. Most scientists believe there is just one giraffe species and nine different **subspecies**, or types, of giraffes.

① Angolan giraffe

⑥ Nigerian giraffe

MAP OF AFRICA

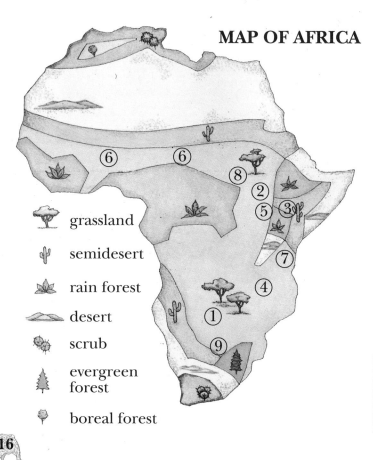

grassland

semidesert

rain forest

desert

scrub

evergreen forest

boreal forest

Match the number of the giraffe to the number on the map to find where each type of giraffe lives.

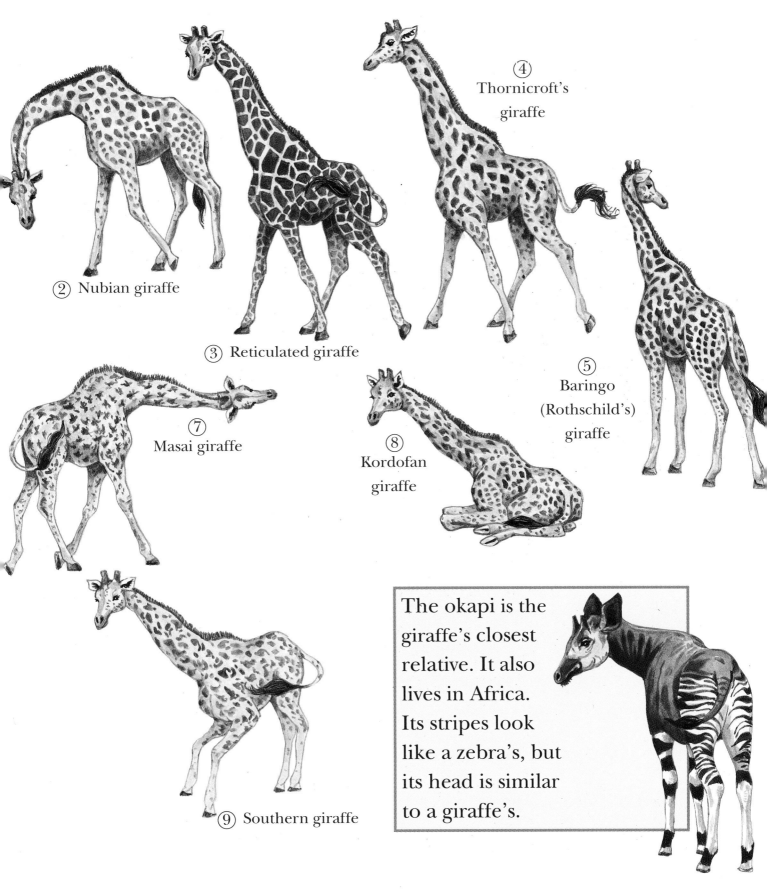

② Nubian giraffe

③ Reticulated giraffe

④ Thornicroft's giraffe

⑤ Baringo (Rothschild's) giraffe

⑦ Masai giraffe

⑧ Kordofan giraffe

⑨ Southern giraffe

The okapi is the giraffe's closest relative. It also lives in Africa. Its stripes look like a zebra's, but its head is similar to a giraffe's.

Herds

A group of giraffes is called a **herd**. A giraffe herd has from four to fifteen members. It may be made up of just bulls, cows and their babies, or cows and babies with a single bull.

The behavior of giraffes differs from that of other animals that live in herds. A member of a giraffe herd may wander away and come back to the herd days later. It may also join another herd. Not all giraffes are part of a herd. Some bulls and older giraffes live alone.

Two bulls may compete to be the leader of a herd by **necking**, or neck wrestling. They twist their necks together and take turns swinging their heads into one another. After a while, one bull gives up. Both giraffes usually escape these contests with only a few small injuries.

On the move

Giraffes are almost always on the move. They spend most of their time walking and sit down for only a few minutes each day. With such a long neck and legs, getting up is difficult! To stand up, a giraffe moves its neck backward and lifts itself up on its front legs. Then it throws its neck forward to pull itself onto its hind legs.

Giraffes have an unusual walk. They move the front and hind legs on one side of their body at the same time. Most animals move a front leg and the opposite hind leg when they walk.

With its long stride, a giraffe can move quickly. It can gallop up to 35 miles (56 kilometers) an hour. Giraffes also step or hop over tall fences and walls.

A giraffe is born

Giraffes mate year-round. Fifteen months after mating, a female gives birth to one calf, as shown in these pictures. She stands up to deliver the calf. After the baby drops to the ground, the mother licks it clean. Soon the calf will stand and drink its mother's milk.

24

Growing up

A newborn calf is the size of a tall person and grows very quickly. It drinks its mother's milk for the first week and then begins eating a few plants as well.

As calves grow, mothers and other females in the herd guard them from predators. More than half of all baby giraffes, however, are killed by enemies. Young giraffes that survive become adults within four to seven years.

Giraffes and other creatures

Giraffes rarely fight with other animals. They often eat near other herbivores such as zebras, elephants, antelopes, and wildebeests. These animals seem to prefer staying close to giraffes because giraffes can spot predators from far away.

The oxpecker is a bird that has a **symbiotic relationship** with the giraffe. Symbiosis is a partnership between creatures of different species. Each animal helps the other stay healthy. Oxpeckers perch on the giraffe's back and remove harmful pests such as ticks and fleas from its coat. They help keep the giraffe's skin healthy and, in return, they are rewarded with a feast of insects.

a flea

Look out for predators!

Giraffes are always watching for predators such as lions, hyenas, and wild dogs. Adult giraffes can usually see and avoid enemies before they are close enough to strike, but predators often kill calves.

If a giraffe cannot escape from a predator, it will fight. The giraffe's powerful kick can knock off a lion's head!

Giraffes and people

Humans are the giraffe's main enemy.
Some people kill them for food. **Poachers**,
or illegal hunters, kill giraffes and sell
their hides and the hair from their tail.
The hair is used to make jewelry.

As towns and farms grow, the giraffe's
natural habitat disappears. Many parks
have been created to protect the giraffe's
territory. Outside these parks, however,
giraffes are still threatened by poachers
and the loss of their home.

Giraffe facts

🍃 Giraffes are seldom noisy, but sometimes they moo, whistle, growl, cough, scream, and even snore!

🍃 Few creatures are born with horns. A calf's horns are soft and flat at birth, but they gradually harden and stand up.

🍃 The hair on a giraffe's tail is as thick as heavy fishing line. Each strand is more than 3 feet (1 meter) long.

🍃 Giraffes cannot swim.

🍃 Giraffes need only 30 minutes of sleep each day. They never sleep more than five or ten minutes at one time. Giraffes can sleep sitting down or standing up with their head and neck lowered.

🍃 A giraffe closes its nostrils to avoid being poked up the nose by needles and thorns on branches.

31

Words to know

acacia tree A tree with fernlike leaves, found in warm climates

camouflage Patterns or colors that help an animal blend into its environment

cud A ball of partly digested food that is brought up into the mouth for rechewing

habitat The area in which an animal naturally lives

herbivore Describing an animal that feeds only on plants

illegal Describing something that is against the law

irregular Describing patterns of jagged spots on a giraffe's coat

live young Baby animals that do not hatch from eggs

mammal A warm-blooded animal that has hair or fur

mate The act of a male and female animal joining together to produce young

mineral A natural substance, found in bones or in the ground, that is necessary in an animal's diet for good health

poacher A person who breaks the law to hunt animals

predator An animal that hunts and kills other animals for food

reticulated Describing patterns of smooth-edged spots on a giraffe's coat

symbiotic relationship A partnership between creatures of different species

valve A fold of skin that helps control the flow of blood through an organ or blood vessel

warm-blooded Describes an animal whose body temperature is constant

Index

2 3 4 5 6 7 8 9 0 Printed in USA 6 5 4 3 2 1 0 9 8